HEINRICH ERNST KAYSL_

(1815-1888)

36 ETÜDEN

FÜR DIE VIOLINE

36 Studies for Violin

op. 20

Revidiert von / Revised by

Hans Sitt

C. F. PETERS

FRANKFURT/M. · LEIPZIG · LONDON · NEW YORK

INHALT / CONTENTS

36 Etüden

⊓ Herabstrich – *Down-bow* – Tirez
V Hinaufstrich – *Up-bow* – Poussez

1———— ⎰ Finger liegen lassen
⎨ *Leave the fingers down*
⎱ On laisse rester les doigts

H. E. Kayser Op. 20

Edition Peters Nr. 3560

10005 I.

Allegretto

3.

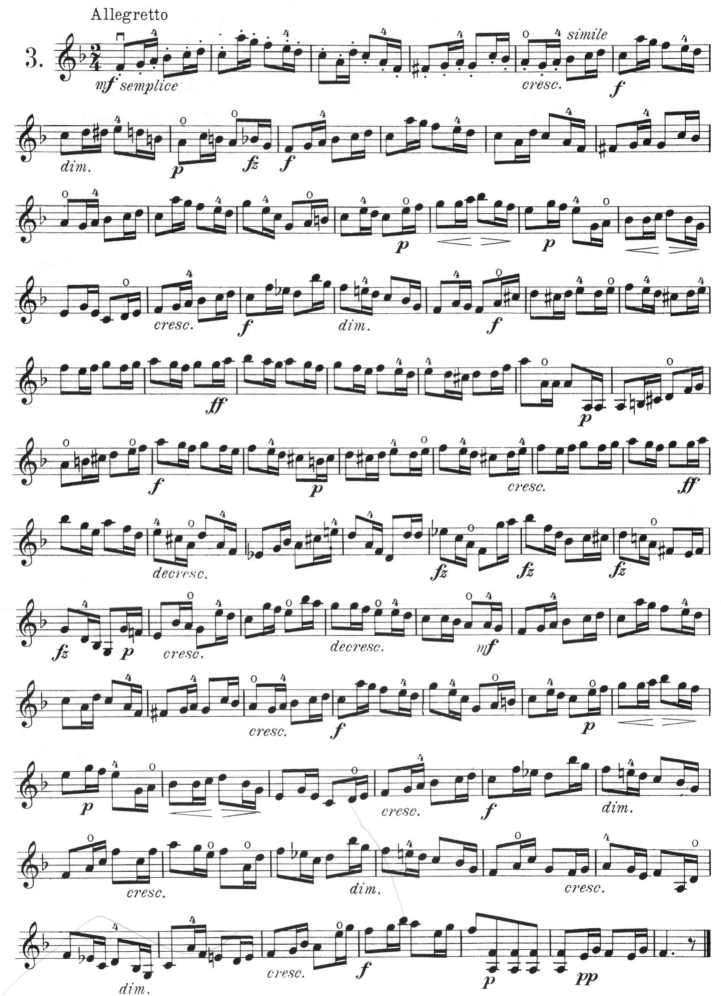

Allegro vivace
5.
f
simile
mf
cresc.
ff
dim.
mf
cresc.
f
dim.
p
mf
cresc.
f
ff
dim.
cresc.
f
mf
cresc.
f
dim.
cresc.
f

8

Allegro moderato

7.

8. Comodo

Arpeggio.

Diese Etüde muß auch, bei völli-ger Ruhe des Ellbogens und richtiger Biegung des Handgelenkes, gestoßen geübt werden.	*Cette étude doit être exercée aussi, avec le coude en parfait repos et une exacte courbure du poignet, staccato.*	This etude should be practised also, with the elbow perfectly at rest and a correct bending of the wrist, staccato.

Allegro, ma non tanto

10.

⊓ Herabstrich - *Down-bow* - Tirez
Ⅴ Hinaufstrich - *Up-bow* - Poussez
1 ⎯⎯ { Finger liegen lassen
Leave the fingers down
On laisse rester les doigts

H. E. Kayser Op. 20

Allegretto

13.

10005 Ⅱ.

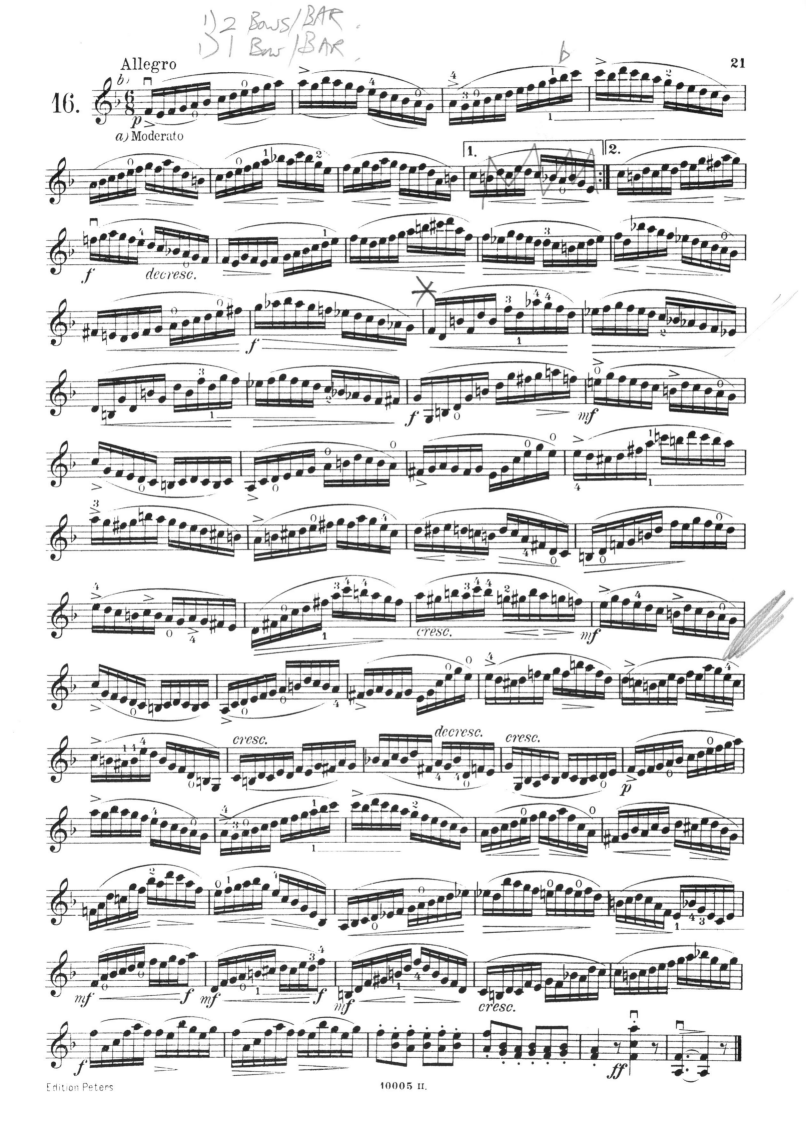

Andante quasi Allegretto
melodioso

17.

Fest und später auch springend
Ferme et ensuite aussi par sauts
Firmly and afterwards also by leaps

Man springe von ⊕ zu ⊕
Sautez de ⊕ à ⊕
Leap from ⊕ to ⊕

Allegro

19.

21.

Allegro

Allegro assai

furioso

24.

⊓ Herabstrich – *Down - bow* – Tirez
∨ Hinaufstrich – *Up - bow* – Poussez
1 ⎰ Finger liegen lassen
⎱ *Leave the fingers down*
⎰ On laisse rester les doigts

H. E. Kayser Op. 20

Allegro

25.

34

27.

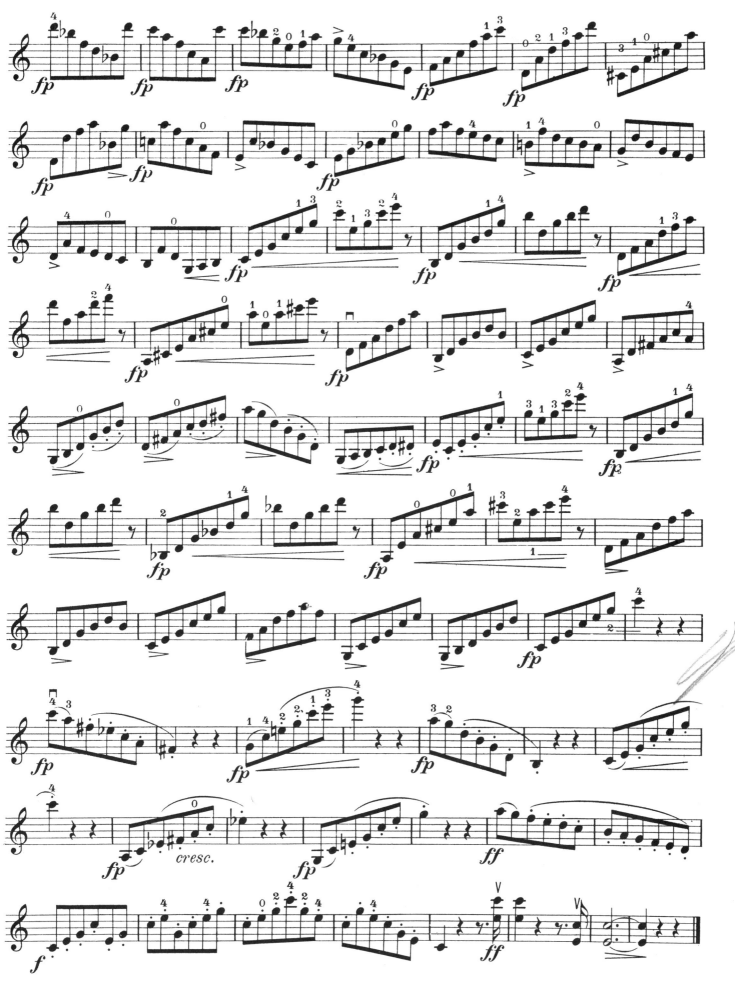

Allegro

29.

10005 III.

Allegro moderato

30.

Allegro moderato

33.

VIOLINKONZERTE
VIOLIN CONCERTOS
Ausgaben für Violine und Klavier / Editions for Violin and Piano

J. S. BACH Konzert Nr. 1 a-Moll BWV 1041
 (D. Oistrach) . . . . (*) EP 4996
– Konzert Nr. 2 E-Dur BWV 1042 (Strub) (*) EP 4593
– Konzert g-Moll BWV 1056 (rekonstr. nach dem
 Cembalokonzert f-Moll) (Schreck/Szigeti) EP 3069a
– Konzert für 2 Violinen und Streicher d-Moll
 BWV 1056 (D. Oistrach) . . . . (*) EP 9032
BEETHOVEN Romanzen G-Dur op. 40, F-Dur
 op. 50 (I. Oistrach/Fechner) . . . . EP 9171
– Konzert D-Dur op. 61 mit Kadenzen (Flesch) EP 189
BÉRIOT Konzert Nr. 1 D-Dur op. 16 . . . EP 2989a
– Konzert Nr. 7 G-Dur op. 76 . . . . EP 2989c
– Konzert Nr. 9 a-Moll op. 104 . . . . EP 2989d
BRAHMS Konzert D-Dur op. 77 mit Kadenz
 vom Hrsg. (Klingler) . . . . EP 3893
BRUCH Konzert g-Moll op. 26 (Menuhin) EP 1494a
CUI Suite concertante op. 25 . . . . Bel 502
GIORNOVICHI Konzert Nr. 4 A-Dur
 (Lebermann/Feldigl) . . . . EP 5922
GLASUNOW Konzert a-Moll op. 82 . . . . . . Bel 195
HAYDN Konzert C-Dur Hob. VII:a 1
 mit Kadenzen (Flesch) . . . . EP 4322
– Konzert G-Dur Hob. VII:a 4* mit Kadenz
 (Held/Thiemann) . . . . (*) EP 9952
– Konzert A-Dur Hob. VII:a 3 mit Kadenz
 (Thiemann) . . . . EP 9953
J. JOACHIM Kadenzen zu den Konzerten von
 Beethoven op. 61, Brahms op. 77, Mozart KV 218
 und 219, Viotti Nr. 22 . . . . EP 9115
LALO Konzert F-Dur op. 20 (Herrmann) . . EP 3796
– Symphonie espagnole op. 21 (Menuhin) . . EP 3797a
MENDELSSOHN Konzert d-Moll (Menuhin) EP 6070
– Konzert e-Moll op. 64 (I. Oistrach) . . . (*) EP 1731
MOZART Konzert Nr. 1 B-Dur KV 207
 mit Kadenz (Jacobsen) . . . . EP 2193e
– Konzert Nr. 2 D-Dur KV 211 mit Kadenz
 (Küchler) . . . . EP 2193f
– Konzert Nr. 3 G-Dur KV 216 mit Kadenz
 (Flesch) . . . . EP 2193 L
– – (Ausgabe D. Oistrach) . . . . EP 2193m
– Konzert Nr. 4 D-Dur KV 218 mit Kadenz
 (D. Oistrach) . . . . (*) EP 9181

MOZART, ferner:
– Konzert Nr. 5 A-Dur KV 219 (Marteau) (*) EP 2193a
– Adagio E-Dur KV 261, Rondo B-Dur
 KV 261a (269), Rondo C-Dur KV 373   (*) EP 3827
PAGANINI Konzert Nr.1 D-Dur op. 6 (Stross) EP 1991
RODE Konzert Nr. 6 B-Dur (Davisson) . . EP 1095b
– Konzert Nr. 7 a-Moll (Davisson) . . . . EP 1095c
– Konzert Nr. 8 e-Moll (Davisson) . . . . EP 1095d
SAINT-SAËNS Havanaise op. 83 (Thiemann) EP 9292
– Introduktion und Rondo capriccioso op. 28
 (Georges Bizet/Thiemann) . . . . EP 9294
SPOHR Konzert Nr.2 d-Moll op. 2 (Davisson) EP 1098a
– Konzert Nr. 7 e-Moll op. 38 (Goethel) . . . EP 8102
– Konzert Nr. 8 a-Moll („Gesangsszene") op. 47
 (Davisson) . . . . EP 1098d
SVENDSEN Romanze G-Dur op. 26 (Schuster) EP 9016
TELEMANN Konzert B-Dur TWV 51: B 1
 (Hobohm/Bernstein) . . . . EP 9039
TSCHAIKOWSKY Sérénade mélanchol. op.26 EP 4333
– Konzert D-Dur op. 35 (D. Oistrach/Mostras) EP 3019b
VIEUXTEMPS Konzert Nr. 2 fis-Moll op. 10 EP 2574
– Konzert Nr. 4 d-Moll op. 31 (Arbós) . . . . . EP 3322
– Konzert Nr. 5 a-Moll op. 37 (Arbós) . . . . . EP 3323
VIOTTI Konzert Nr. 22 a-Moll (Klingler) . EP 1100a
– Konzert Nr. 23 G-Dur (Davisson) . . . . . . EP 1100b
VIVALDI Ausgew. Konzerte aus op. 3 „L'estro armonico"
– – Konzert G-Dur op. 3 Nr. 3 RV 310 . (*) EP 9453a
– – Konzert a-Moll op. 3 Nr. 6 RV 356 . (*) EP 3794
– – Konzert E-Dur op. 3 Nr. 12 RV 265   (*) EP 4379
– Konzert G-Dur op. 7/II,2 RV 299 . . . . . . EP 9838a
– Konzerte op. 8 „Die Jahreszeiten" (Kolneder)
– – Nr. 1 Frühling RV 269 . . . . (*) EP 9055a
– – Nr. 2 Sommer RV 315 . . . . (*) EP 9055b
– – Nr. 3 Herbst RV 293 . . . . (*) EP 9055c
– – Nr. 4 Winter RV 297 . . . . (*) EP 9055d
– Konzerte ohne Opuszahl:
– – Konzert B-Dur („Posthorn") RV 363 . . . EP 9139
– – Konzert d-Moll RV 245 . . . . EP 9058
– – Konzert d-Moll RV 237 . . . . EP 9463a
– – Konzert A-Dur („Pisendel") RV 340 . . . . EP 4207
WIENIAWSKI Konzert Nr. 1 fis-Moll op. 14 EP 5504
– Konzert Nr. 2 d-Moll op. 22 . . . . EP 3296

(*) zu diesen Ausgaben ist eine CD mit eingespieltem Orchesterpart erhältlich / (*) Music partner CD with recorded orchestral part available

C. F. PETERS · FRANKFURT/M. · LEIPZIG · LONDON · NEW YORK
www.edition-peters.de · www.edition-peters.com